DADDY'S BIG SECRET

Jordan Learns the Truth

JERMAINE K. SEAMON

Co-author

JORDAN K. SEAMON

Illustrated by
SRI JUNI

FIREBRAND PUBLISHING
ATLANTA GA USA

© 2021 Jermaine K. Seamon/ Jordan K. Seamon
All Rights Reserved.
No part of this publication may be reproduced, stored in a retrieval system, or transmitted, in any form or by any means, electronic, mechanical, photocopying, recording, or otherwise, without the written permission of the author.
Published by Firebrand Publishing
2870 Peachtree Road
Atlanta, GA 30305 USA
www.firebrandpublishing.com

ISBN: 978-1-941907-39-9

This book is a work of fiction. Places, events, and situations in this book are purely fictional and any resemblance to actual persons, living or dead, is coincidental.

Printed in the United States of America.

Forward

I love my Dad very much and he means a lot to me! I am excited to help my Dad share this book with the world, like he decided to share a part of himself with me. My Dad has shared so many things with me that it was hard to find out that he did not tell me about his "Big Secret." I know our story can help other families.

Forward By:

Jordan Kristine Seamon (daughter)

11 years old

One spring Saturday morning, my Parents and I were walking to the Free Library of Philadelphia to return some of my books. My Dad and Mom were walking with me side by side, holding my hand. I was singing a new song that I'd heard and my Dad asked me,

"Where did you hear that song?"

"I heard it from a TV show that I was watching just last week with Mommy. It was about these two friends that were in a dancing show. One of the girls had a disease called diskia," I said.

My dad asked, "Jordan, do you mean dyslexia?"

"Yes, that's it, dyslexia! The girl in the show said that she was afraid to tell anyone, or talk about it, "I replied.

Dad asked, "So, then what happened on the show?"

"I am not sure, Daddy. I didn't watch the rest of the show, but Daddy, could she die?" I asked my dad afraid.

My mom answered before my dad could, "No, she won't die baby."

I turned to my mom, "Can anyone get dyslexia?"

"Yes baby, anyone can be diagnosed with dyslexia. If you are dyslexic, it just means that you learn a little bit differently," replied Mom.

I became more curious, "how can you tell who has dyslexia?"

My mom thought about it before answering, "Well, there is no way to tell by sight if someone has dyslexia. Teachers like Mommy often notice it by looking at a person's writing or hearing them read aloud."

I immediately started asking more and more questions about dyslexia. My Mom kept responding, but my Dad was just listening.

We stopped right in front of the library. We were a little early, so we waited for the officer to come and open the door. My Mom and I were still talking, and my Dad stepped in front of me and kneeled down, looked into my eyes and said,

"Jordan I have something to tell you."

"Yes, Daddy," I replied.

"I am dyslexic, I have dyslexia."

I was shocked. "You do, Daddy? Are you alright? Does it hurt?" I asked.

I grabbed my Father's face with both of my hands, holding his face in concern. I began looking deep into his eyes, as if I could see right through him.

Dad laughed and said, "Yes, I am fine sweetheart and no, it doesn't hurt."

"Maybe his face does now!" said Mom, laughing.

My Daddy smiled with delight, as he looked up at Mommy.

He looked back at me and continued, "Dyslexia is a learning disability. I have difficulty sometimes with spelling, reading and writing."

My Daddy stood up, took my hand and we walked into the lower level of the library. We sat down in the children's section.

I looked at my Dad and asked, "Daddy, why didn't you tell me? I have a lot of questions."

Daddy sighed and said," Yes Jordan, I know... I know you have questions and I will answer all of them. When I was younger I was always afraid to tell anyone that I was dyslexic because I thought that they might make fun of me, so I hid it so people would not think that I was not smart. I hid it for a very long time."

I asked, "How did you get it?"

"I was born with it," said Daddy.

"Does Mommy have it too?"

My Mom answered, "No, Baby."

"Daddy, do I have it?" I asked.

"No, Baby, I was identified by my teachers. They saw that my reading accuracy, fluency, and writing skills did not match my grade level."

"Daddy, why were you born with dyslexia?"

"I can't say why I was born with it. Sometimes we will have differences that start from birth, or that come about later in life. I just remember that I was identified when I was younger, and I was told that I had to take special classes. I believe I was in the fifth grade when I began going to my special classes. I always loved school, but it was hard for me back then."

Suddenly it seemed like we were all transported back in time, to when my father was an elementary school student.

Dad started telling me his story. He said, "I remember sitting in the classroom at my school, and going to my different classes, especially my English class. My Teacher would say, *'Good Morning class. Please open your vocabulary books and turn to page ten; everyone will get a chance to read some of the passages aloud.'*

We would begin to take turns reading, no more than two to three sentences at a time, until we completed all of the passages.

I could feel the fear creeping up my back, like a very large spider, as it got closer and closer to my turn to read aloud in the front of the class. I would suffer in silence. I did not tell anyone how I felt.

Finally, my Teacher would say, 'Ok Jermaine, it's your turn. Please start at the first paragraph on page eleven.'

My hands would begin to sweat. I would say and read words that did not appear on the page that I was reading. I would start to stutter, while reading over words, because it appeared that the letters would move around like jumping beans.

The amount of time that it should have taken me to read two minutes of sentences, would take me four to five minutes. It seemed like hours. I could not wait to hear my teacher call on another student. I would breathe a huge sigh of relief when the reading assignment was over and I could sit down."

I felt so badly for my Dad, "Daddy, that sounds like it was really scary. Did you feel like that for every class?"

"I would feel like this during all of my classes. Our teacher would give us new spelling words. We had to define each word and come up with sentences for each of them. At the end of the week, we would have a spelling test. We would have reviewed these words all week in class and for homework."

"Daddy, that's just like my tests. Was it hard to study your spelling words for the test?"

"I would study really hard at home for the test, but when it was time to take the test on Friday morning, I would freeze and it would seem like time stood still. I couldn't remember how to spell any of my spelling words."

"Wow, so you failed the test even after all of that studying, and you had to go through this in every class?," I asked.

"Yes, being dyslexic affected all parts of my learning. I found it hard in any class that involved reading, and math was also a little difficult. I had to figure out how to learn in a different way so that I understood my classes."

My mom looked at me and said, "Jordan, that is why Daddy always tries to make sure that you understand your school work. He remembers how difficult it was for him until he got the help that he needed."

"Yes, that's right. I would feel like I had to ask the teacher so many times for help, I would be embarrassed among all my friends. I felt as if they might laugh at me because I needed so much help."

"Mommy and I would never laugh at you Daddy."

"Thanks, Baby, I know that you wouldn't," said Daddy smiling.

My mom said, "That's right Baby! Your Grand-Mom and Pop-Pop were also very helpful to your Daddy. They gave him loads of love and support."

"My parents wanted to help more so they got a tutor who would come to my house after school. Along with my special classes, tutoring helped a lot. In fact, your Pop-Pop gave me my first Batman comic book. I would look at the pictures and I was determined to try and read along. This helped me in my struggle with reading because I was seeing more words and became excited about reading something that I really liked."

"That is awesome!" I said, "Is that why you like comic books so much?"

"Yes! I would read comic books every chance I got. My teachers even allowed me to read them in my special classes. Reading became less frightening for me. I was also given more time to write down my lessons and my teachers would help by going over it more than once."

"Daddy, so did school get any better?"

"I used the tools that I learned in my special classes and started to get A's and B's on my report card, not D's and F's. I was very proud of myself, but I was still very uncomfortable sharing my dyslexia with anyone. I thought that it was easier to keep it to myself."

"So you kept it a secret?," I asked.

"Yes, I still kept it a secret. When I got to high school I began to play football and worked really hard to keep my grades up because I loved playing. My Father asked my Aunt Crystal to tutor me in Math and English, and that was also a great help."

"Oh wow, that's great!"

My Dad smiled, "Aunt Crystal would help me to understand my homework assignments. She was a huge help in getting me through high school successfully, and gave me the courage to know that I could go to college."

My Mom said, "and that is where Mommy and Daddy met, at Cheyney University of Pennsylvania."

"Yes, 'You too, can meet your Boo at CU!'," said Daddy smiling.

"That's funny Daddy! I remember when Mommy became a teacher at Cheyney, and the students would say that all of the time. It's amazing that both of you graduated from Cheyney and were able to work there after graduation."

Mom said, "Yes, it is amazing that we met there. I remember when your father came over and helped me with the issues that I was having with the computer in Browne Hall."

"That was when I was a student, completing work-study under Mrs. Baldwin and Ms. Box. They allowed me to help others, but I was getting just as much help with my classes while I was there," said Daddy.

"I can see why you decided to keep your dyslexia a secret because it was really hard, but I am glad that you told me. It seems like you feel a lot better talking about it now than you did back then?," I asked my Dad.

"Yes Jordan, that's why I want to be able to help children who may be going through the same challenges that I have experienced."

"I guess there could be students in my classes who are going through the same thing?" I said.

"Yes, and it is a constant fight for them every day. I still have to work at reading and writing every day. There are people who have no idea about my dyslexia. I always felt like I had a secret identity."

"Yes, It's like you are a superhero! And you had to fight dyslexia, the bad guy! Awww Dad, that's great! So, Mommy and I are your sidekicks?"

Daddy smiled, "My sidekicks! Yes, that's a great way to look at it. Both of you are pushing me to be better because I still need help and have to find new ways to improve my skills every day. I use my difference as my strength. Now you know Daddy's Big Secret!"

Dedication:

I want to dedicate this book to the one who has been the wind beneath my wings since we first met, my Wife Felicia. With her words of encouragement and powers of persuasion, she has motivated me to be a little better every day and to transform perceived weaknesses into my greatest strengths. This book is a labor of love, with help from my wife, who inspires me to live and work for something greater than myself Through her love for me, I have found courage and power in my words.

Selected Bibliography

The International Dyslexia Association - https://dyslexiaida.org/definition-of-dyslexia

The International Dyslexia Association offers the following definition of dyslexia:

"Dyslexia is a specific learning disability that is neurobiological in origin. It is characterized by difficulties with accurate and/or fluent word recognition and by poor spelling and decoding abilities. These difficulties typically result from a deficit in the phonological component of language that is often unexpected in relation to other cognitive abilities and the provision of effective classroom instruction. Secondary consequences may include problems in reading comprehension and reduced reading experience that can impede growth of vocabulary and background knowledge."

ABOUT THE AUTHOR
JERMAINE K. SEAMON

Jermaine Keith Seamon is a Philadelphia, PA native. He currently lives in Atlanta, Georgia.

Jermaine has been married for 16 years to his beautiful wife Felicia, and they have one daughter Jordan, who is now 14 years old.

Jermaine is currently a police cadet for the DeKalb County Police Department. Jermaine holds a Bachelor's Degree in Social Relations and a Master's Degree in Adult and Continuing Education (both) from Cheyney University of Pennsylvania.

Since graduating from Cheyney, Jermaine's vast experience in community service stems from work transitioning homeless youth at Covenant House of Pennsylvania, preparing teen fathers within the Males Achieving Responsibility Successfully (MARS) program under Communities in Schools of Philadelphia, as well as improving the quality of life for veterans and recovering addicts at Open Arms Transformation Center in Coatesville, PA.

Jermaine is currently working on his second book, and is excited to finally share his first book, "Daddy's Big Secret" with the world. Jermaine also has a monthly blog on everything comic books and superheroes called, "The Comics Analyst" at https://www.seamonent.com.

www.ingramcontent.com/pod-product-compliance
Lightning Source LLC
Chambersburg PA
CBHW040758240426
43673CB00014B/386